MW00389074

This book belongs to:

____

Made in the USA
Middletown, DE
21 December 2021

56818881R00066